Evolving Your Hair Business into 7 Figures with the 7-figure Hair Boss

22 steps to assist with running a successful hair company.

Jaylon Aaron

Evolving your Hair Business into 7 Figures with the 7 figure Hair Boss: 22 Steps to assist with running a successful hair company.

Copyright © 2018 by Jaylon Aaron

ISBN 978-1-943284-24-5 (pbk.)
ISBN 978-1-943284-25-2 (ebk)

A2Z Books Publishing
Lithonia, GA 30058
www.A2ZBooksPublishing.net
Manufactured in the United States of America
A2Z Books Publishing has allowed this work to remain exactly as the author intended, verbatim.

Introduction

It's 1:00 am and I just got in from a 4-hour filming of my reality show Chasing Atlanta. I have to wake up early in the morning to meet with my contractors for my up and coming hair store and beauty salon, and after that meeting I have to rush back home and start packaging up and mailing out hair, because I got over 2000 orders this week and we all know, no one wants to wait for their hair so that means no sleep for me for the next few days.

Hi, my name is Jaylon Aaron and I am a Celebrity Stylist, the inventor of the "3 Part Sew In", a beauty mogul, and also known as the 7 figure hair boss. I started doing hair when I was 15 years old and knew instantly that this is where my passion lies. I opened my first salon with no loans or grants, but from standing on my feet for sometimes 3 days and doing 50 clients in one-time span and from my discipline, I am now 23 years old and have built an empire.

However, over the years while building my business I learned quickly that everything was not as easy as it looked and wish someone had given me the tea on the hair business before I started. I get hundreds of DMs a week of people asking me how to start a hair business or a flat iron business, or even an online business period. I'm always giving out tips, and advice and I even sell hair and beauty vendors. So, I decided to put it all in one place to help others who want to start a hair or online company. In the evolving your hair business into 7 figures book, I will give you 22 steps that will help you build your very own beauty/online empire.

Jaylon Aaron

Table of Contents

Step 1:
Who wants it?

When I first started my business I thought everyone was going to be my customer and I found out very quickly that no matter what business you are in, EVERYONE is not and will not be your customer.

Jaylon Aaron

The 1ˢᵗ step in evolving your hair business is identifying your target market. Just in case you don't know what a target market is: it is a group of people or individuals a company sells its products to and who it will market and promote to when it is time to gain exposure for the product.

When getting into the hair market, you need to identify exactly who you will be selling your hair to because that will determine:

- ✓ What types of hair you will need to sell. (For example, hair for white women or hair for black women)

- ✓ What prices you need to sell your hair for. (For example, under $50 a bundle or over $150 a bundle and this should be based on what you can afford)

And

- ✓ How and where you will market. (For example: on Instagram through paid promos or through Facebook with a group.)

Some people like expensive hair, some people like the middle grade or the middle of the road hair and some people don't want to spend a lot of money on hair, so they opt for something inexpensive. So when figuring out who your target market is and what they want, you must ask yourself where do I want to fit in, in that particular market.

You need to ask yourself and answer:

- ✓ Do I want to sell high-grade expensive hair that only a few people can afford?

- ✓ Do I want to sell middle-grade hair that most people can afford?

Or

4

- ✓ Do I want to sell inexpensive cheap hair that everyone can afford?

And please note that the quality of the hair is not always contingent upon the price of the hair. Because I sell very good quality hair and my prices are what some would consider inexpensive, however, I have found really good vendors that give me really good prices so in the hair business or any business in general, remember that you always want to get the most bang for your buck.

These are the mistakes I've made because I didn't have someone to inform me, so now I'm telling you.

Additionally, if you can't decide what you want to sell, think about yourself as the customer and if you were your customer, think about your hair shopping habits, where you go to purchase hair, and what types of things you like.

If you have a hard time deciding who your target is, conduct a poll, ask your friends, family members, and people who you think might be your customer and ask them what type of hair they like, what they will pay for it and where they currently go to buy hair. Analyze all this information and decide who your target market will be.

Notes

Step 2:
What is it?

When I first started selling hair I can admit, I did not know what I was doing. I had no idea how many different types of hair were out there, so I started doing some research and purchasing different types of hair and making a decision based on what I liked. I wanted to learn everything about the hair that I would be selling, so if any questions were asked I would know how to answer it.

These are the mistakes I've made because I didn't have someone to inform me, so now I'm telling you.

Jaylon Aaron

The 2nd Step in evolving your hair business is figuring out what type of hair you are going to sell. In Step 1, you identified your target market which is who you will be selling your hair to, but now it is time to decide exactly what type of hair will you be selling and getting to know your product.

There is nothing worse than someone who is selling something that they do not know anything about, so when becoming a hair boss or a boss in general, you need to know all the ins and outs of that industry and what you will be selling.

For example:

There are different grades of hair:

- Grade A
- Grade AA
- Grade AAA
- Grade AAAA
- And so on.

There are different textures

- Peruvian'
- Brazilian

- Malaysian

You have different patterns like:
- Straight
- Body Wave
- Deep Wave
- Curly

Then you have the lengths
- 18-22inches
- 24-26 inches
- 28-30 inches
- 30 inches and longer

And the addons:
- Closure
- Frontals etc,

Get to know your different types of hair. Buy some, wear it, wash it, color it, and do everything the customer would do. And if it is something you love, then that is your product, if not, do not sell it.

Notes

Step 3:
What do you Call it?

Back in my younger days, I always knew I wanted to see my name in lights, so it became second nature for me to name my business after me.

Jaylon Aaron

The 3ʳᵈ Step in evolving your hair business is creating a boss name for your hair company. Your company's name is just as important as the type of hair you will carry and the brand that will be built because the name is what the company will go by and what will be on everything including your:

- Website
- Packaging
- Stationaries
- Business cards
- Social media pages
- Legal paperwork

And any and everything that has to do with the business. Therefore, your hair company's name should be something that you will love and something that is brandable (will talk about branding later in the book).
When coming up with your hair company's name think about the longevity of your company and think about what name will sound good today and also sound good 10 years from now if you are still in business.

Some people name their hair companies after themselves, while others name their hair companies after other things like the city where they are from or just random or generic names that they like. And there is no right or wrong answer here since this is your company, however, when coming up with the right name of your hair company, there are a few things that you will need to consider which are:

- Making sure the name fits with the brand identity.
- Making sure the name is catchy but not too trendy since trends do not last.

- Making sure the name is memorable, easy to say and understand.
- Making sure the name looks good in print, because it will be printed on everything.

Additionally, when creating your hair company's name, think about it like naming your child. You want it to be something you will be proud of and something that provides some insight into the company. If you have a hard time coming up with your hair company's name, enlist the help of your peers.

Notes

Step 4:
Where can I Find it?

I must admit I didn't' know how different it would be to sell hair online, but I knew in order to get where I am I needed to do both. So I did.

Jaylon Aaron

The 4th Step in evolving your hair business is deciding where you will sell your hair (or product) and how your customers will receive their hair (or product).

The last thing you want to do is have your customers looking for your products and how to purchase it because if it is too hard to find, believe me, they will go somewhere else.

You have to decide if you will:

- Sell your hair online through a website.

- Sell your hair online through social media.

- Sell it at a physical location like having your own boutique, salon, or kiosk at the mall.

- Will you sell it wholesale to other salons or hair sellers?

- Have a combination of places where your hair can be purchased.

If you decide that you want to have a physical location like your own hair boutique, you must consider:

- Where you will have this boutique and is it a great location based on your target customer.

- Will you rent or purchase a place and will you find it on your own or enlist the help of a real estate agent.

- How much can you afford to pay and how much will it cost you monthly.

If you decide that you want to sell your hair online via a website and/or social media, you must consider:

- If you will be filling orders on your own, hiring someone, or hiring a company.
- If you will use a drop shipping company that will mail out the hair for you.

Because the one thing that customers hate to do is wait for their hair. You want to make the purchasing process as easy as possible whether it is through your website or in your store. Create a purchasing process that is seamless and ensure your customers can get the hair they want and when they want it.

Notes

Step 5
Where's the Paper?

I knew from the start I wanted to start a legitimate business, so I knew what had to be done in order to do that. Get my paperwork together! There is nothing worse than someone claiming to be a boss with an unregistered business!

Jaylon Aaron

The 5th Step in evolving your hair business is ensuring that you are a legally functioning business. Anyone can buy hair and sell it out of the trunks of their car, but if you want to run a real business and become financially secure, you will have to have real paperwork to show.

Here is what you will need:

- You will need to reserve your business name in your state to ensure that no one else uses it.

- You will also need to register your business with the state that you reside in with either an LLC, Corporation or whatever suits your business need.

- You will also need to obtain an EIN (Employee Identification Number) also known as FEIN (Federal Tax Identification Number), which is like a Social Security Number for your business that allows you to do things like open up a business bank account, merchant services account, and pay federal taxes (if this applies to your business).

- You may also need to obtain a business license in order to sell some products and also in order to purchase some products wholesale.

Additionally, you may need to obtain a seller's permit if you will be charging state taxes, in which you will be obligated to pay back to the state in which you reside and are charging taxes.

I recommend hiring a business coach, consultant, and/or lawyer about the exact paperwork requirements you will need. You can also contact the small business administration office in your city and they should be able to help you with all the questions you have.

Notes

Notes

Step 6:
Who are the Resources?

I knew that without the right hair plug, I was not going to be successful.

Jaylon Aaron

The 6th Step in evolving your hair business is finding the right vendor. Finding a vendor which is often referred to as the plug, is one of the most important things you will do for your business because this is where the product you will be selling is coming from.

When choosing a vendor you want to make sure that you ask all the right questions for example:

- How long will it take for products to ship because having a long wait time for products can cause customers to become impatient which could potentially ruin your brand.

- What is the guarantee and return policy because often times, vendors and especially if they are overseas, do not have quality control and may sometimes send out bad batches of hair. You want to make sure that if this is the case that you will be able to return or exchange products otherwise you will end up with merchandise that you cannot use.(NEVER send customers bad hair)

You also want to ask vendors:

- How much are the products, are they discounted if you buy in bulk, and what can be done to get better deals in the future because when building a hair company, you want to ensure you are getting the best products at the best prices so that you can pass those savings down to your customers.

- How do they gather their products and what processes and procedures do they take to ensure you are getting quality merchandise.

Additionally, you will need to create effective lines of communication with your vendor and make sure that what you expect is understood and what they expect is understood.

You can purchase vendor lists from a number of avenues, like other hair companies on social media and YouTube or you can research and find some yourself, the main thing is to make sure they have the type of product you want and will be happy selling.

Notes

Step 7:
Who's Checking?

Jaylon Aaron

The 7th Step in evolving your hair business is creating some type of quality control within your business. In case you do not know what Quality control is; it is the process of making sure that the product and in this case the hair is good quality.

Have you ever purchased hair that looked one way online but when you got it, it looked like something totally different? Well, that happens quite often in the hair business and almost everyone who has a hair business has gone through this one time or another.

In Step 6, we talked about choosing a great hair vendor, but that is only one part of creating a 7 figure hair company. The quality of your product must be immaculate and in order to ensure that it's the best quality, your product must be checked. There are thousands of hair companies out there and if your product is not good, believe me, you will lose that customer and more than likely, you will not get them back. No one wants to feel like they have gotten bamboozled or scammed out of their money because they paid for something, but received something else. There are many hair companies online and on social media that are doing this and not caring about their company's hair brand or their reputation.

If you are marketing a certain quality of hair, then that is what you need to sell. If the product is not something that you would use, then why would you sell it to your customer? There is ONLY one way to ensure that your product is good quality and that is to check every single item before sending it out.

As stated, you can do your own quality control, you can hire a team or some friends and/or family members that you trust to do it or you can hire a quality control company and let them check your products. Create a list of must-haves (for example thick luxurious hair) and things that you do not like (for example smelly hair that sheds) and use that as your checklist for your quality control. I know it may sound like a lot of work but when creating a 6 or 7 figure business, you cannot cut corners especially with the quality of your products.

Notes

Step 8:
Where's the Money?

Money is my friend and she knows it, so at all times I need to know how to get her and where to find her!

Jaylon Aaron

The 8th Step in evolving your hair business is figuring out how you will receive your money. Nothing is more unprofessional than customers not having a way to pay you. We will talk about creating a website in a later step, but in this step, we will discuss creating payment systems.

By now you should have an EIN# and if you don't, you will need to obtain one (IRS.GOV or ask around for assistance) in order to open up merchant services and business bank account. And know that no matter what payment processor or system you choose, your money has to be allocated to a bank account so there is no way around this.

You can open up a business bank account with the regular banking chains like:

- Wells Fargo

- Bank of America

- SunTrust

- Or even your local Credit Union

Please note a lot of the big chains do not like working with hair companies so definitely do your research.

And if you open up an account with any of these companies, they will walk you through the process and usually require a least $100 down to open a business bank account. They will also assist you with the Merchant Services Account, which is how credit card payments will be processed.

Once you have the business and merchant services account together, then you will decide which payment system you will take for example:

- PayPal
- Stripe
- Square

Please note a lot of the merchant services do not like working with hair companies do your research.

Some people are even using Apps like:

- Cash App
- Apple Pay
- Zelle

So my recommendation for you is to do your research, ask a lot of questions to make sure what you choose is right for you and your business and create an easy way for your customers to pay you.

I went through tons of merchant services because I had too many sales and the bank basically stated that my company was a risk because of that matter. I now use PayPal and it's the best way to do your tracking numbers, track, and dispute. With PayPal and setting up the count, you just have to be sure to let them know what you are expecting them to make as well let them know that you will be using PayPal shipping services.

These are the mistakes I've made because I didn't have someone to inform me, so now I'm telling you.

Notes

Step 9:
What's the Charge?

I love a bargain and know that everyone including the rich love when they can save money, so when I created my business I wanted to make sure that everyone that wanted my products could afford to buy it.

Jaylon Aaron

The 9th Step in evolving your hair business is creating your Pricing Strategy. In case you do not know what a pricing strategy is: this is the process of creating the prices of your product. This is important because the way you price your product is how your company will be seen as a brand.

Some hair companies price at a premium, which is where the prices are high and some companies price at a discounted rate, which is where prices are low. And then you have companies that price somewhere in the middle.

You should determine the prices of your product based on your target market (customer), the quality of your products, and the brand you will be building. Think about the amount of money you will have to invest in your business and what you want to be seen as in the industry.

For example:

- Do you want to be known as the premium company that has expensive, but very high-quality hair?

Or

- Do you want to be known as the budget hair company that sells cheap hair, but it is still of good quality?

Or

- Do you want to be known as the good quality hair company that sells great hair at a great price?

Some people double the wholesale price of the hair and make that the retail price while others add $20 or $30 to the wholesale price of the hair and make that their retail price. There really is no right or wrong answer, so think about your desired end result (how much money you want to make) and conduct your industry pricing research before creating your pricing strategy.

Notes

Step 10
What's the Brand?

When creating the Jaylon Aaron Brand, the first impression I wanted to make on my customers was "The element of surprise." I wanted them to love the price, but be blown away when they saw how luxurious the product was.

Jaylon Aaron

The 10th Step in evolving your hair business is creating a Branding Strategy for your company. Branding is making your hair company recognizable and the things that will set your hair company apart from others.

In order to create a branding strategy for your hair company, you will need to create a set of long-term branding goals that will assist you in building your brand.

You will need to:
- Identify what is your purpose for being in business
- Identify your mission and vision.
- Identify what emotional connection you will have with your customer.

You can also build your brand and assist with creating your branding strategy by:

- Creating a Brand image (we will discuss this in the next step), that aligns with your company's core values and will attract your customer and will include things like:
  o Your hair company's logo and website
  o And all the visuals associated with your company.

- Identifying your brand's message that will speak your hair company's language and also speak directly to your customer and include things like:
  o Your hair company's tagline
  o The overall perception the customers have of your hair company.

It's important to create your hair branding strategy because you want your brand to be perceived in a certain type of way and without putting the time in to build your brand, you cannot grow your business. Think about some of the successful brands like; Starbucks and Mac or Chick Fil A and Nike. These companies spent the time building their brands and you must do the same.

Notes

Step 11:
What does it Look Like?

Jaylon Aaron

The 11th Step in evolving your hair business is identifying and creating your brand's image and message. A brand's image and message is the impression that your customers will have when they think about your company.

When building a hair brand, you want to ensure that you are creating something that is unique and innovative and is what your customer would be drawn to. For example, let's say you were trying to choose brand colors for your hair company but your target audience was older sophisticated women. A color like pink or purple pretty and also youthful, would not be a brandable color for your company. However, a more sophisticated color palette would be gold and black. Now, on the flip side, what if your target customers were young girls or ladies, then the pink and purple colors would work.

Additionally, when creating your brand image, think about an adjective you would use to describe your company based on what you want your customer to feel and think when they see or purchase something from your company.

- Do you want them to think luxury?
- Do you want them to think fun?
- Do you want them to think pretty?
- Do you want them to think cheap?
- Do you want them to think sophisticated?

So, when creating your brand's image, you want to ultimately think about the target customer and what it is that they will be drawn to. When you create your logo, website, social media, marketing materials and all visual aids, think about the fonts and pictures used and make sure it aligns with your adjective.

If you have a hard time creating your brand's image, you should contact a banding expert (branding coach & strategist) that can assist you because the one thing that will hinder you from creating a successful hair company is a poorly created brand.

Notes

Step 12:
What's the Symbol?

I love my Jaylon Aaron logo and when people see it, I want them to automatically think luxury hair.

Jaylon Aaron

The 12th Step in evolving your hair business is creating or getting a professional logo. Having a great logo is a part of branding and definitely a part of your hair company's image. A logo is a symbol or a graphic of some sort that represents the brand and is needed in order to be taken seriously as a company. Some people make logos on their own, but that is not recommended if you are not a graphic artist. You will want something professional because you will use you your logo on:

- Your website
- Your packaging
- Your social media pages
- Anything that will be visual and represent your company.

When creating or getting a logo created, you want to make sure that you :
- Find someone professional to create it for you by researching the market and seeing what type of work you like.
- Use the Brand colors because you want your audience to think about your company when they see those colors.
- Use the Brand message because you want your visuals and product that the logo will be used on to speak their language.
- Test it before making it official because you do not want to use something that will make you look unprofessional.

Your logo should represent you and your hair company and make a huge impact on your target audience from the first view and if you think about my Brand Jaylon Aaron and a few other beauty brand logos like Sephora, Loreal, Clinique, Cover Girl, and even Olay, you can see that we all use the name of our company, used sophisticated fonts and sleek colors to create our logos. So there is a formula that works for beauty companies.

You can use that formula or create one on your own, but make sure you get a professional logo created.

Notes

Step 13:

What's Your Website?

When I ask someone who claims to have a business for a website address and I don't automatically get it, I think to myself; this is NOT a real boss.

Jaylon Aaron

The 13th Step in evolving your hair business is creating or getting a website created. And although you may be building your hair company and brand on social media, you must have a website for your customers to purchase products from. Because what will happen if Facebook, Twitter or Instagram decides today that they were going to shut down? What would you do? Would your customers have a way to get in contact with you or will they have to take their business elsewhere. So remember that EVERY Business needs a website.

I have seen lots of companies come and go and one of the main reasons they do not last is the lack of visibility. Visibility means being visible in numerous places and on numerous platforms, but the main platform is your website.

You can hire someone to create your website & purchase your domain as well or you can create one on your own. There are tons of platforms that you can use for your company for example:

- Shopify (commonly used for hair companies)
- Squarespace
- WordPress
- Wix
- Word Press
- 3dcart
- Volusion
- Etc.

Make sure your website is professional and includes:

- Your logo and brand's message
- A clear description of what you do and sell
- Professional images
- Correct Prices
- An easy checkout process
- Contact information

Notes

Step 14:

What's Your Instagram?

Right now I have almost 300K followers on Instagram and I started out with a few just like everyone else. I worked my brand to get to this point, but my ultimate goal is 1M + followers! Watch me Work!

Jaylon Aaron

The 14th Step in evolving your hair business is Creating a Social Media presence. In Step 13, we discussed creating a website and we also discussed being visible. Having your hair company on social media will make you more visible.

And I know first hand about visibility because I was able to build a 7 figure business from social media. This is not something that happened overnight because it took me years to build my brand, however, if you want to be successful, you must cover all avenues.

According to research, 90% of small business owners and marketing individuals indicated that being on social media increased traffic to their websites by over 80% and as stated, I know this to be true because of the company I built.

My recommendation is to create at least one social media business account for your hair business, but you have a few options to include:

- Instagram
- Facebook
- Twitter
- SnapChat
- LinkedIn
- Pinterest
- And a few more

You want to post things about your business, you want to post products that you have, you want to post sales, and you also want to post information about you because believe it or not, most people who build successful hair brands were able to do so because their customers bought into them and their lifestyles, more than the hair. And no, you do not have to be rich or to be the prettiest person in the world, but what you post has to be authentic. Your customers want to know that you are real and you represent your brand. So be cognitive of what you post on your social media pages.

Notes

Step 15:
Who did that Packaging?

Never judge a book by it's cover is one of the oldest sayings, but I do not believe that especially in business. I believe that the average person and thing is judged by its outer appearance. This may not be the case in every business, but this is what has worked for me.

Jaylon Aaron

The 15th Step in evolving your hair business is creating professional packaging. Packaging for your hair is important because it ties in with the company's brand image and message and should be taken very seriously.

Your packaging will differentiate you from your competition and will be one of the main tools for marketing your hair company.

Your packaging choice should be made based on your:
- Budget
- Your Branding Goals

Your packaging can include things like:
- Hair Bags (Satin, Silk Etc).
- Hair boxes
- Labels
- Mailers

Your packaging should be professionally done and include things like:
- The Brand colors
- The Brand logo

Do your research, ask lots of questions, and choose a company that can work based on your budget and the requirements you want. Ask about minimums because you do not want to purchase more items than you need especially when getting started.

Here is a list of places you can go to get packaging for your hair business:

- Uline

- eBay

- AliExpress

- Paper Mart

- Efavormart

- And there are a lot more on Google.

Notes

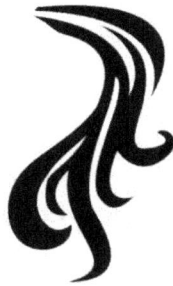

Step 16:

What's Your System?

I love when things run smoothly, especially in my business!

Jaylon Aaron

The 16th Step in evolving your hair business is setting up systems within your business. Have you ever purchased hair from a company or any product period and you knew instantly that the company was unorganized? Well, I have and to tell you the truth that used to be my business. We were unorganized and some days we didn't know if we were coming or going.

I did not know about systems when I first got started, but once I learned about them, my business was able to flourish and I became a boss.

These are the mistakes I've made because I didn't have someone to inform me, so now I'm telling you.

In case you do not know; a business system is a set of methods created so that a business can run smoothly and in a hair company, this is definitely needed. Otherwise, you will not be running the hair company, the hair company will be running you.

With a hair business system, things will be:

- Automated

- Delegated

For your hair company I recommend:

- Automatic emails to customers after purchasing.

- A certain time frame for hair to be shipped after purchase (for example; some people ship hair once a week, while I ship 48 hours after purchase).

- A certain mailing process (for example; drop shipping from a dropship company or printing out shipping labels and creating packaging as soon as the order comes in).

- Sending our tracking numbers for packages as soon as you have them.

- A turn around response time for emails, DMs etc. (for example, I check my emails and DMs 3 times a week and always respond to clients within 72 hours. We will discuss more in the customer service section).

- A certain time to purchase hair and make it automatic as well (for example, I buy hair twice a week and I have a vendor that knows my general order. If I need more because sometimes I run specials, then I would order more but no matter what happens, I order hair twice a week to make sure I ALWAYS have what I need in stock).

Create systems within your business.

Notes

Step 17:

Who is on Your Team?

I started out working by myself because that was all I could afford to do, but when I got my coins up, I put my team together and that was one of the best things I ever did.

Jaylon Aaron

The 17th Step in evolving your hair business is putting together a team. You can start off by doing everything on your own and this is probably best when you are getting started and do not have a lot of money, but as your business grows, you will need to enlist the help of others.

You heard of the trade "a Jack of All Trades is a Master of None," well, you do not want that to be you in your hair business. You want to shine in the area that you are good at and in this case that should be selling hair.

These are the mistakes I've made because I didn't have someone to inform me, so now I'm telling you.

When it is time to enlist the help of others, there are a number of things you can do.

- You can hire someone fulltime to assist you.

- You can hire someone part time to assist you.

- You can barter services with someone to assist you. (for example, you can enlist the help of a friend or family member and give them hair instead of money in exchange).

- You can hire an intern and pay them a fraction of the cost or let them work for free for college credit hours.

- Or you can do a combination of these.

You will need assistance with :

- Packaging

- Mailing

- Customer Service

- Marketing

- Branding

- Quality Control

- And whatever other things that will need to be done in your business.

Do NOT try to do everything yourself because if you are all over the place in your business, your customers will know and this will be a big turn off. My favorite saying is, in order to be a boss, you must be the boss.

Notes

Step 18:

Who Can I Call?

When jumping into the hair business, I did not know how important customer service was, and not just regular customer service, but good customer service. In the hair industry, you are dealing with a lot of women and when dealing with women, you must be willing to deal with their emotions as well. I had to learn not to take certain things personal in order to be successful in my business.

These are the mistakes I've made because I didn't have someone to inform me, so now I'm telling you.

Jaylon Aaron

The 18th Step in evolving your hair business is Customer Service. Customers are the most important thing in your business because without customers you won't make money and without money, you can't stay in business.

You should know that customer service within all industries is important, but in the hair industry specifically, it is vital. The reason is that there are so many variables in the hair industry that can occur which can affect your business, so how you handle it will be the determining factor in you being successful or not.

Here are a few scenarios:

- Sometimes customers are messy and just want to start something because they either do not like you, what you represent or they just don't have anything else to do.

- Other times customers have real issues with products and just want their voice to be heard.

- Often times it can be a combination of the two and figuring out how to deal with it is the key.

Customers in the hair business will do things like:
- Post bad hair reviews on social media.
- Tell their friends and family not to shop with you.

- Tell their banking systems that they didn't authorize the charge or never received the item and it ends up being a chargeback.

So when you have situations like this, it is best to:

- Stay Calm
- Stay Professional
- Come up with the best solution if it's speaking to the customer directly and seeing how the situation can be resolved.

I recommend :

- Having a 24 to 48 hour response time on all business inquiries.
- Having resolution options readily available.

Remember, that in your business, you will be the best representation of your brand and no matter what happens, always remain professional. Know that some bad things are going to occur, but make sure that your customer service stays A1 at all times. The best brands have the best customer service.

Notes

Step 19:

Who's Loyal?

"I Love a Mercedes Benz. That is one of my favorite brands of all times when it comes to cars. The reason is, I feel exquisite and luxurious when I drive it, I feel like everyone is looking at me when I pull up and I know that there is a little bit of envy in those that cannot afford to buy the brand."

Jaylon Aaron

The 19ᵗʰ Step in evolving your hair business is creating a demand and loyalty to your brand. This is not the easiest thing to do, but in order for you to stay in business, people must want what it is that you are selling.

I know people who buy Jordans faithfully, and I know people who only drink coffee from Starbucks, hell even my grandmother is loyal to Tide laundry detergent. So what this means is that these companies have created a demand for their brand and brand loyalty.

In order for a hair company to do this, you must be willing to create an organic connection with your customer almost like a relationship and you can do this by:

- Making sure your brand seems exclusive (like the people who are part of it are part of a club or something).

- Speaking your customer's language (we discussed this in identifying our brand).

- Provide something better than your competition.

- Make your customers feel like they cannot get what you provide anywhere else.

Notes

Notes

Step 20:

Where are we Marketing?

If you know me, you know I take every minute I can to market Jaylon Aaron hair and products. Some people hate it, but hey what can I say, I am a walking billboard and we all know you don't get a second chance to make a first impression, so in my eyes why not make it and market it at the same time.

Jaylon Aaron

The 20ᵗʰ Step in evolving your hair business is to create a marketing strategy and be very aggressive with your marketing. Marketing is different from branding. Branding is basically a representation of what you stand for.

In the hair business, there are many ways to market, but you should:

- Make your marketing efforts geared toward your customers.
- Choose things that will highlight your business
- Market within your budget.

Because often times, we see what others are doing and think we can do the same thing and in all reality, each business should have its very own marketing strategies and marketing goals.

Some people market the old school way which are:
- Word of mouth and referrals
- Handing out flyers
- Mailing out
- Purchasing a billboard spot

And others market new school which are things like:
- Social media posts
- Social media ads
- Commercials
- Email marketing
- Creating sales funnel

Additionally, you need to think about things like what will you use when marketing for example:

- The product itself
- Pictures or images of the product
- Celebrity of lifestyle expert endorsements.

You can also:

- Collaborate with other businesses
- Have events
- Join hair competitions
- Go to hair or trade shows
- Create how to's and post on social media or create a YouTube channel

And think about the items you can use to market by adding your logo or slogan to it for example:

- Water bottles
- Tshirts
- Clothing
- Hats
- Junk drives
- Etc.

Overall, marketing your business will be the most important thing you will do to evolve it to the next level. Always take every opportunity you can to market your company and always have a business card, flyers, and even product samples available.

Notes

Step 21:
Who can I Connect with?

One thing that I learned in business is to create good and strategic business relationships and partnerships.

Jaylon Aaron

The 21st in evolving your hair business is to create partnerships and collaborations. And not just any partnerships or collaborations, but some that make sense to the growth of your business.

When I first got started and was opening up my first salon, I tried to do everything on my own, but being so young there was a lot that I didn't know. So I had to learn and sometimes even lean on other beauty professionals for their advice.

All advice is not good advice, but one sure way to build your business and brand is to attach yourself and your company to someone or something that can help.

- Sometimes people have a bigger following that you can use.
- Other times they have knowledge and expertise that you can use.
- And sometimes they have both.

But realistically in order for someone to want to partner or collaborate with you, you must be bringing something to the table as well. No one wants to work with someone they see as an opportunist so if given a chance to work with or collaborate with someone, make sure you do your part.

There are many ways you can partner or collaborate for example:
- Having joint events.
- Creating a product together.
- Posting about each other.
- Etc.

And if you do not know how to approach someone that you might want to consider working with, draw up a professional letter and email it or DM and get the ball rolling.

You never know if you do not ask, and you will be surprised at how working with others will keep you inspired, motivated and on the right track to evolving your business.

These are the mistakes I've made because I didn't have someone to inform me, so now I'm telling you!

Notes

Step 22:
How to Start with no Money!

Anything you want to achieve you can, you just have to believe.

Jaylon Aaron

The 22nd and Final Step of evolving your hair business is to show you how to get started with no money. At first, I wasn't going to add this step, then I thought about how I got started and have helped others get started with little to no money so I definitely needed to add this step.

You may be wanting to start a hair company, but do not have money to start it and if you have done your research then you know that on average, people invest upwards of $5000 to get started selling hair, however, without spending a dime on hair you can actually start.

Here are the steps:

1. You will need to find a hair vendor that can either drop-ship or ship hair within 24 to 48 hours.

2. You will need a website so you can either pay for one or make one for free on platforms like Shopify or bigcartel and on your website you will add that hair ships in 5 to 7 business days to give yourself some wiggle room to get the product to your customer.

   a. You can use pictures you got from the hair vendor or stock photos until you have money to take pictures of the hair yourself for your website.

3. You will price the hair based on your pricing strategy, but make sure you are earning a profit.

a. For example: If you pay $29 for a bundle of hair wholesale and you price this bundle at $79 on your website, then you will earn $50 a bundle.

4. You will market your hair via free avenues (social media, friends family etc.).

5. Once customers have purchased the hair on your website, you will take that money and buy the hair and keep the profit or reinvest.

6. Once hair is ordered, you will either have it drop shipped to the customer or you will manually ship it yourself.

So by telling the customer that hair ships within 5 to 7 business days, you have time to get the hair, inspect the hair, package the hair (if you want to), and ship to the customer. This way the customer pays for the hair even before you have the hair and you can use this process indefinitely if you do not want to store inventory. Also, do not think that you are doing something wrong because this is totally an acceptable business practice. A lot of the big corporations do it and this is an easy way to start your business if you have little or no funds, but want to get started right away.

Notes

Letter from the Jaylon:

Congratulations on completing the Evolving Your Hair Business into 7 figures book. Finishing this book is the first step to growing your business and brand. With these 21 steps, I hope I have given you the tips, strategies, and techniques you need to take you and your business to the next level. I shared some of my stories and experiences good and bad with you because I want you all to win and avoid some of the mistakes I made. I wish I had a resource like this to help me when I got started, but unfortunately, I did not. As a result, though, I thought as a mogul and successful business owner it was my duty to provide the knowledge I have learned over the years and pass it on to the next generation of young business owners. I hope you enjoyed it and good luck to you with all of your business

Thanks

Jaylon Aaron

Contact Info

jaylonaaroncollection.com

Order book online at amazon.com and all other online distributors

Interested in Writing and or Publishing a BOOK???

Contact : Dr. Synovia @www.A2ZBooksPublishing.net

www.ingramcontent.com/pod-product-compliance
Lightning Source LLC
Chambersburg PA
CBHW071458210326
41597CB00018B/2596